a Mouse in the House

A Short Story by Steve Tarpinian

Illustrations
by
Steve
Dansereau

For permission requests, write to the publisher at SlippedAway.org/contact.html

More information about Steve Tarpinian, as well as information about his memoir, can be found at SlippedAway.org

Some names and identifying details have been changed to protect the privacy of individuals.

Book design and illustrations by Steve Dansereau.

Printed in the United States of America

ISBN 978-0-692-06685-0

Library of Congress Control Number:

2018933363

www.SlippedAway.org

FOREWORD
by Jean Mellano

In 2012, Hurricane Sandy devastated countless human lives, many of whom are still recovering in 2015. Steve (the author) and I considered ourselves very lucky; the only damage we sustained was a tree falling and destroying our back-yard shed.

There are also many untold stories of how non-human species were adversely impacted by Hurricane Sandy. One such story is of mice that sought refuge in our home. Steve and I believed that the mice were also casualties of Hurricane Sandy, as we thought they must have fled from our shed in terror to the closest safe place—our house. These mice inspired Steve to write the true story, *A Mouse in the House*.

The lesson in this story is to show compassion. Some of us are more fragile than others and need to be handled with care. Showing compassion is not a sign of weakness. It is a sign of great strength of character and a powerful human spirit. Steve showed great compassion for the little critters in this story. He had a great capacity for love and compassion for all living beings in his life. That is what made him a giant among men.

This book is in memory of Mike Stewart, a great friend who always had a shoulder for me to lean on in my times of greatest need.

"You can easily judge the character of a man by how he treats those who can do nothing for him." - Author Unknown

I had seen mice in the pet store.

These little creatures were adorable and on sale for only ninety ninety-cents each. They were small, and seemed to be sleeping all over themselves. They were extremely cute.

"What a good pet they could make," I thought to myself. "They're small, quiet, vegetarians and smart!"

Then I realized I had no extra time to devote to any pets in addition to the two rescued rabbits Jean and I owned.

What was I going to do with a mouse anyway? Take him for a run? Teach him how to swim or ride a bike? Oh well, I said good-bye to the little fellas and hoped they did not end up being fed to someone's snake. I didn't think about mice again until Hurricane Sandy.

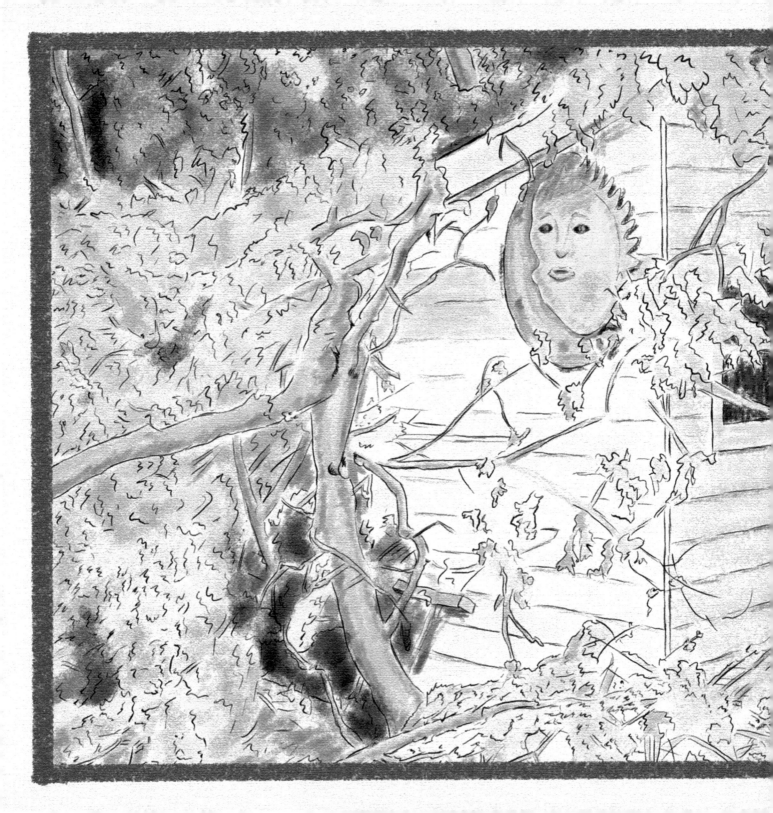

There were many devastating stories two days after the hurricane when I returned home from a trip. Luckily there were not a lot of fatalities, but thousands of people were left without a home they could live in and hundreds with literally no home at all. One sad story I heard was of a woman who, as she was closing her door to the rising water saw several small mice swimming towards the door trying to get in. I never asked if the woman let the little guys in, frankly I didn't want to know. That made me realize how many little animals were also displaced. Sad story, but with so much to do helping friends clean up after the storm and stay warm with no heat and electricity at our home, I did not dwell much on the story of the swimming mice.

We were very lucky. The only damage at our house was from a big tree that fell from a neighbor's yard and took down one of our trees on its way to crushing our cute little shed. Our neighbor Danny was so worried about it that he would fix it for us and get the tree removed. We assured him we were not worried one bit and he need not worry. He was relieved and we were happy to see him smile. He has always been a terrific neighbor and friend to us for over ten years.

As the days passed, things started to get a little crazy with gas lines forming at the gas stations, an unexpected snow storm and delays on getting power and cable service back to hundreds of thousands of homes like ours. These natural disasters tend to bring out the best and worst in people. Some people had fights on gas lines while others opened their homes to neighbors and friends. A friend of ours named Josie was staying with us since her condominium was flooded. Ironically, it was Josie's neighbor who told her the story of the mice trying to swim to her door.

As the weeks passed by, life slowly started to get back to normal. The gas lines receded, people were starting to return to their homes, but it seemed to go very slowly. One day, I went into the kitchen in the morning and saw a small black "thing" scurry into the bottom of the kitchen cabinet. I say black "thing" since I really feel like all I saw was a tail wiggle around and then disappear.

I froze in place wondering if I really saw this or if I was still asleep and imagining it. I knelt down to see where it went and sure enough, in one corner of the cabinet there was an open space where there was no wood about three inches wide. I was now convinced that I saw a mouse as he ran back into his hiding place. Was there a mouse in the house? Should I tell Jean and our houseguest Josie? I let them know what I saw and the mystery mouse became a daily topic of conversation.

A few days later Josie left us a note that said, "I think the mouse ate some of this bread". Jean and I looked and saw a small tear into a paper bag that had some bread in it and a small bite was missing. In addition, we saw a few small droppings on the counter. Jean was angry and said now they are invading our space and eating our food. We have to do something. I said "oh what's the harm" and she explained to me that they can carry all sorts of disease and multiply and so on.

The next day, as Jean and I were discussing how we would handle this problem, Josie told us that she saw the mouse as well. That day we also found more evidence of the rummaging they were up to when we found a wrapper from a chocolate bar all torn up and wedged in one of our stove burners. And there was another problem - Josie described a white and brown mouse, and I saw a black one. We no longer had a mouse problem we had a mice problem!

That was the last straw. Jean said they have to go.

We decided we would get mousetraps and I said I would take care of the task the next day. It was a very busy day of work with meetings and driving around, phone calls, etc. I told a neighbor, Bob, that we had a mouse problem and his response was go to Home Depot to get some mouse traps. Although I felt reassured I could get the right things to take care of the problem, I knew he was not talking about anything close to humane. I was off to buy traps to rid us of the mice. My phone rang as I was entering Home Depot and it was Jean asking if I got the traps yet and to get humane ones. I assured her I would do my best to get humane traps and that I was walking in to get them at that very moment. After getting the other supplies I was there for, I asked a Home Depot employee where I could get mousetraps. He said row nine and as I started to walk in that direction he said "make sure you get the old fashioned ones, the humane ones don't work". I looked over the shelves trying to see if there were any humane options. They all looked and sounded lethal. I was running out of time and settled myself to the fact I was getting the ones that will solve the problem. Off I went, made my purchases and headed home.

As soon as I got home, Bob and I went to work putting peanut butter on the traps and setting them in the cabinets and on the floor where we had seen the mice. Jean asked if the mouse would suffer and Bob said no, not at all. Then when she left the room, he leaned toward me and in a soft voice said, "they usually do not die right away and the box will flip around, so you just take them out and "finish them off". Great, I get to be the one to grab the mouse twisting in pain and take him out to "finish him off".

That evening, while having dinner, the subject of these traps came up. Jean wanted to be sure that if we hear one in the night that I would get up and take care of it. The reality that the traps would kill the mice had settled in, and I realized that I am not okay with that.

I started to do a search on the computer for humane traps. As with anything else, there is a wealth of information on the Internet for trapping mice. I found all types of traps and their reviews. It appeared as though some of them do work.

A few sounded like they were not much better than the killer ones but I did find one that was a large metal box and had two openings that the mice can go in, but once in, they can't get out. The description said it can trap up to thirty mice! I called the local Ace and Home Depot stores. It was now 8:30 PM. I was running out of time and at any moment I might hear the snap of the trap just a few feet away from me. A store nearby that closes at 9:00 PM said they have the trap I want in stock. I asked Josie and Jean, who had just finished eating dinner and were looking over my shoulder while I was researching, if we should run out and get this trap.

It was unanimous. I got ready to go, Jean took the inhumane traps away and washed off the peanut butter, and Josie said she will take a ride with me. Thirty dollars later we were checking out of the hardware store and on the way home.

We loaded the trap with three whole wheat crackers, some gourmet peanut butter, and cheese. There were holes in the side of the trap so the aroma of these delicacies could waft out and attract the mice. Ah, relief, we could all sleep knowing we were not going to hear a "snap" and come in to see a dead little animal in the kitchen.

The next day we decided to call an exterminator to get a professional opinion of how to handle mouse infestation. That afternoon, a very knowledgeable and nice guy from a large company that handles all sorts of critter infestations (mice, rats, squirrels, raccoons etc.) took a flashlight and searched around the area where we saw the mice. The exterminator found another area with some evidence of mice activity (in other words, droppings) under the stove. He then took a walk around the house to see if there were any areas that mice could come in from the outside. When he returned, he sat down to give us his results and suggestions for handling the situation. The exterminator advised us to seal off some small exterior openings where a mouse could gain access to the house.

After a few days with no takers in the trap and no sign of mice we started to wonder if they had left on their own. We had, however, spoken with many friends and acquaintances that had dealt with mice in the past and not one of them told us that the problem was solved without having to trap them, or worse, "finish them off".

A few days later, I had some trouble sleeping and sat up in the living room watching TV. I thought I heard a rattling in the kitchen. I muted the TV and there was silence. I started to fall asleep so I went back into the bedroom. A few hours later one of our rabbits started thumping. We also heard some more rattling in the kitchen. Jean and I headed to the kitchen and there was no noise.

I decided to take a look inside the trap with a flashlight just in case there was a mouse and every time he thought we were around, he stopped stirring. Sure enough, I saw two little eyes staring back at me!

"We caught one!" I shouted, "and it's a baby!"

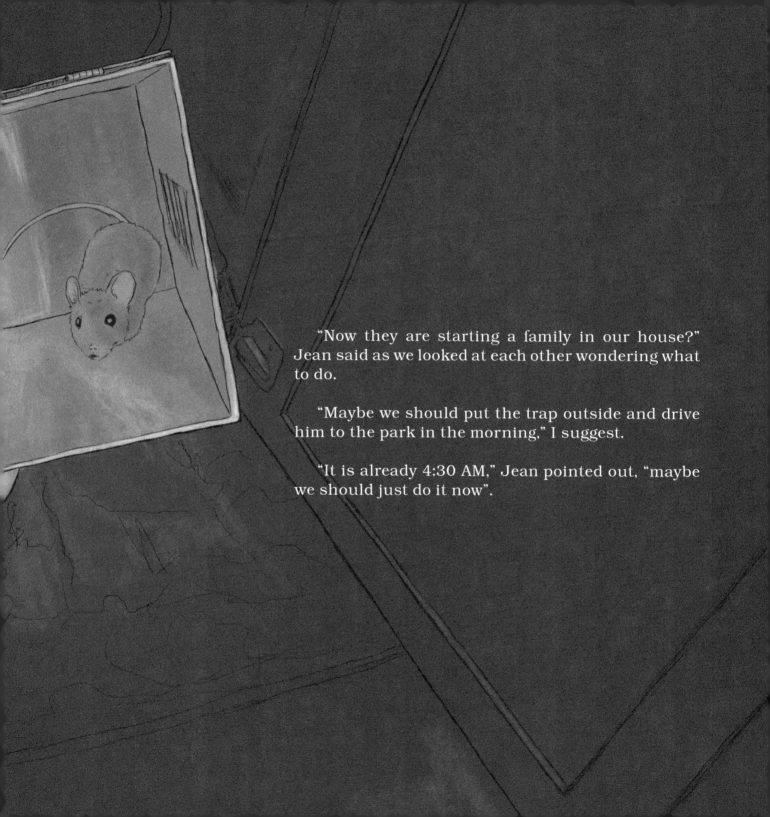

"Now they are starting a family in our house?" Jean said as we looked at each other wondering what to do.

"Maybe we should put the trap outside and drive him to the park in the morning," I suggest.

"It is already 4:30 AM," Jean pointed out, "maybe we should just do it now".

The next thing I know, we were in the car heading to a park that is exactly one and a half miles from our house. We needed to go more than a mile away, since the exterminator told us that if you take a mouse less than a mile away they would usually come back to the same house! We drove into the park, which was lit up from all the organizations doing recovery for Hurricane Sandy. It was surreal; lit like daytime and no one there.

We parked by the roadside near some bushes. I took the trap and set it down on the grass and as I slowly opened the trap the cutest little mouse was staring back at us and looking very scared. He took a few steps toward us, stood up and seemed to be staring right at us. Jean said "Hi Peanut!" Then after a few more seconds he jumped out of the tin box and scurried into the hedges.

We got in the car and I said to Jean that he was too small and probably will not survive. She said, "Sure he will, he is a field mouse and belongs outside."

"I hope so," I told her, but inside, I felt he was just too frail. We both felt good he at least had a fighting chance, and headed home.

The next day we had a second exterminator come over. He smiled when we told him the story of Peanut. He said we did the right thing to have the entry points around the house closed. He also had some other types of humane traps and sold us three of them. Now we had not one but four humane traps set up and ready to catch more mice.

Days went by and nothing.

Maybe they were on to us?

Maybe they saw Peanut get caught and left town?

Not so fast.

A day or two later, I was out and received a message on my phone from Jean telling me that we caught another mouse in the new trap. Another baby!

On the message she asked me to come home and help her take care of it as soon as I could. I had a few meetings and the whole time I was thinking about how we could keep the mouse, maybe not as a pet, but at least for awhile, and at least until he can get bigger and stronger before we set him free to meet up with Peanut.

A few hours later, as I was finishing up my last meeting, Jean called and said, "Pipsqueak is really cute! How are we going to handle releasing him?"

Pipsqueak? I thought, this is not good, he now has a name and Jean is getting attached. "Maybe we should keep him," I suggested.

"No way!" she exclaimed - immediately followed by, "but if we do, make sure you get a wheel or something that he can exercise on."

Man, talk about mixed messages! She evidently looked up mice as pets online and they need things like that. "Don't worry," I tell her, "I have a plan and will be home in an hour."

Plan? What plan? I have no plan. I simply know that I do not want to toss another little baby out in the now freezing weather to try and find his brother or sister and food and probably be chased and maybe caught by some wild cat or other predator. Mice are like rabbits in that they are prey animals. I stood in the parking lot getting ready to get in my car, and as I lift my head I notice a pet store.

That's the solution! I would go in and buy a small tank and we can keep the mouse for a few days, feed him and make him strong and then release him. I went in and spent forty dollars on a tank, screen top and an exercise wheel.

Ten minutes later, I was at our front door ringing the bell. Jean opened the door and said, "Oh no, you didn't."

"Oh yes I did."

We quickly went into the kitchen and transferred Pipsqueak to the new tank with some fresh hay, a toilet paper tube and the wheel. He ran right into the tube. We wondered if he was going to figure out how to use the wheel. We put a cracker with peanut butter and a bottle cap with water in the tank and went to bed.

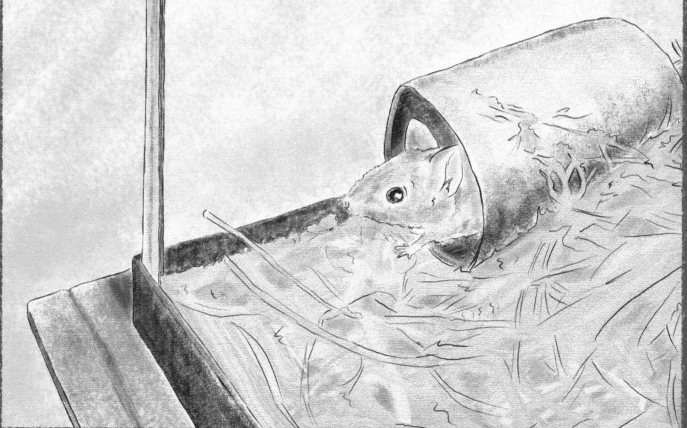

In the middle of the night I got up to get a drink and take a look in on Pipsqueak. As I approached the tank I could hear the wheel spinning!

Darn, in less than twelve hours, the food was gone and he was "in training". As I got close, he stopped and stared at me. This is what I saw - Pipsqueak after his first workout session!

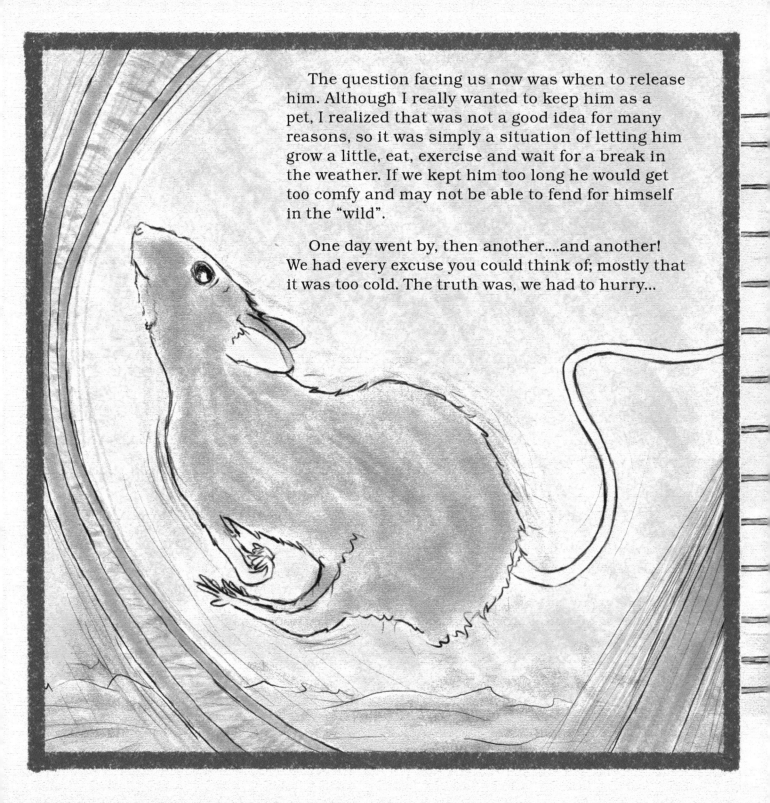

The question facing us now was when to release him. Although I really wanted to keep him as a pet, I realized that was not a good idea for many reasons, so it was simply a situation of letting him grow a little, eat, exercise and wait for a break in the weather. If we kept him too long he would get too comfy and may not be able to fend for himself in the "wild".

One day went by, then another....and another! We had every excuse you could think of; mostly that it was too cold. The truth was, we had to hurry...

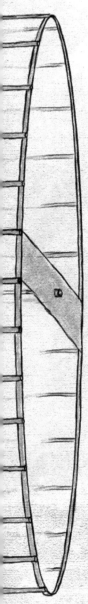

...because besides
getting too comfy
with the gourmet
peanut butter
and whole-wheat
crackers, he was
growing so fast that
he was not fitting in
his exercise wheel
anymore!

When he did his exercise now, he would get tossed out after a few
turns since his body was starting to span almost a quarter of the wheel.

Finally, after about four days, the sun came out and the weather warmed to about forty five degrees. It was time. We took the tank and drove over to Cedar Creek Park. We went to the same exact spot we released Peanut about two weeks earlier. Josie came with us and I slowly tilted the tank on its side. Pipsqueak hid in the hay for a little while, then he slowly started to walk out and once in the grass, darted into the hedges where we left Peanut.

Our fantasy is that he found his sibling and Peanut and Pipsqueak are frolicking around and enjoying the great outdoors.

And our mouse problem? It has been over two years and we have not seen another mouse in the house.

We kept the tank, just in case another one comes and we decide to put him in the "catch and release" program that goes on here at our little house in Wantagh, New York.

"*Pipsqueak*"

ABOUT THE AUTHOR
by Jean Mellano

A Mouse in the House personifies the kindness and gentleness of Steve Tarpinian. Steve was a man of many talents—he was an electrical engineer, a coach, an athlete, a visionary business man, and an author. However, the true and lasting legacy of this man was his humanity.

In 2015, Steve Tarpinian passed away at the age of fifty-four. Before he left this earth, Steve positively impacted so many lives. His kind spirit and good nature was apparent to all who met him. He gave so much to so many with no expectation of a return. It wasn't just human beings that experienced Steve's compassion. He was so sensitive to the fragility of the weaker among us and valued all life, whether it was insects that ventured into our home, a baby bird fallen from its nest, our two rescued domestic rabbits or the mice in this story.

Steve was a gift to all of us; a gift that was only ours to borrow.

For more about Steve's life visit www.SlippedAway.org

Steve and Budgie Bunny

Steve and Snoopy Bunny

Also by Steve Tarpinian:

The Triathlete's Guide to Swim Training
Essential Swimmer
Water Workouts: A Guide to Fitness, Training, and Performance Enhancement in the Water
Triathlon Training: Swimming
The Resurrection of an Armenian Girl

CPSIA information can be obtained
at www.ICGtesting.com
Printed in the USA
BVHW020515080720
583137BV00004B/314

9 780692 066850